Palette in the Kitchen

CELEBRATION EDITION

Favorite Recipes from New Mexico Artists

Originally compiled by Constance Counter and Karl Tani
with an introduction by Vincent Price

SANTA FE

Cover art by Kris Hotvedt

© 2003 by Sunstone Press. All rights reserved.

No part of this book may be reproduced in any form or by any electronic or mechanical means including information storage and retrieval systems without permission in writing from the publisher, except by a reviewer who may quote brief passages in a review.

Sunstone books may be purchased for educational, business, or sales promotional use. For information please write: Special Markets Department, Sunstone Press, P.O. Box 2321, Santa Fe, New Mexico 87504-2321.

CELEBRATION EDITION

Library of Congress Cataloging-in-Publication Data:
Counter, Constance.
    Palette in the kitchen / originally compiled by Constance Counter and Karl Tani ; with an introduction by Vincent Price.—Celebration ed.
      p. cm.
   ISBN: 0-86534-283-0 (paper)
   I. Tani, Karl. II. Title.

TX715 .C859 2000
641.5—dc 21   00-032990

Published in
SUNSTONE PRESS
Post Office Box 2321
Santa Fe, NM 87504-2321 / USA
(505) 988-4418 / *orders only* (800) 243-5644
FAX (505) 988-1025
www.sunstonepress.com

CONTENTS

Introduction	8
Pablita Velarde	11
Douglas Johnson	12
Fritz Scholder	13
Bettina Steinke	14
Elmer W. Schooley	15
Roger d. Schultz	16
Donald B. Anderson	17
Ann Moul	18
Jim Harrill	19
Kris Hotvedt	20
Joseph A. Chavez	21
Megan Lloyd Hill	22
Constance Counter	23
Robert Ewing	24
Peter Hurd	26
Chuzo Tamotzu	27
Miriam & Seymour Tubis	28
Cliff Harmon	29
Harold Fore	30
Sam Scott	31
Swazo	32
John Philip Wagner	33
Helen Hardin	34
Wesley Rusnell	35
Hon. Dorothy Brett	36

37	Nick Abdalla
38	John De Puy
39	Dennis Larkins
40	Charlotte B. Bruce
41	Jim Wood
42	Bernique Longley
43	Henriette Wyeth
44	Barbara Vom Lehn
45	Janet Lippincott
46	Ford Ruthing
47	William Lumpkins
48	Agnes Sims
49	John Meigs
50	Abu Bakr
51	R.C. Gorman
52	Cynthia Bissell
53	Richard Maitland
54	Glynn Gomez
56	Harriett M. Sutton
57	Cecil Howard
58	Rini Price
59	Jean Promutico
60	Margaret Herrera Chavez
61	Forrest Moses
62	Ruben E. Gonzalez

INTRODUCTION

That Greek artist who centuries ago painted so realistically that the birds pecked at his painted grapes may have been inspired to the perfection of his art to preserve his supper!

Chardin, master of still life and simple family man, painted what his wife and children ate—and then he painted them, their fresh French faces flowing with life as surely as the fruits and meats and vegetables inside them.

Lautrec made dainty menus, works of art, for ladies of easy virtue, but, artist at the stove as at the easel, he could follow up a planned seduction with a succulent dish learned from his ancient family in Toulouse.

A few examples of the practicality of this often-thought wastrel breed, the artists. I have never met one who did not savor food and few who could not do their will on it to make it at least seem better than it might have been. Surely there is some definition of all art here, even mine, the ultimate make-believe.

Artists love to eat and eat well—all truly civilized people do—but they are creative in cookery and always personal. They love the stuff from the ground up and there's the difference, "the respect," which to misquote Hamlet, avoids the "calamity of so long life."

What a dull world of food we Americans have been forced into. Perhaps Andy Warhol made that comment with his soup can. The artist, being life's greatest lover, loves food as nourishment for the soul as well a the body, but because the corporeal artist is only as well-fed as his spirit, he sees to it that the fodder, the fuel, is inspired too.

Food is functional for sure, but it can lighten life and lift us from the heavy task of locomotion; it can levitate and let fly the imagination... the artist's product functions for his earthbound brothers in the same way. Art, artist and food are reciprocal.

PABLITA VELARDE

Indian Bread Pudding

1 loaf white bread, toasted
1 cup raisins
1/2 pound butter
3 cups sugar
4 cups water
1 pound longhorn cheese
Cinnamon

Place toast in layers, sprinkling sugar and cinnamon and raisins and cheese (slice cheese in small pieces) on each layer until all ingredients are used.

Use a large skillet and caramelize the sugar. After it is melted, add water and make the syrup. Be very careful because it spatters and you might burn yourself. Add the ½ pound of butter to hot syrup and pour over the bread layers. If bread seems too dry, add a little more water. Stir a little and put in the oven at 350° for 30 minutes.

Photo – Barry Aguilar

Kneel Down Bread
(Navajo Recipe)

"I learned to make this bread while living with Navajo Indians on their reservation here in New Mexico. Since living in Cerrillos, N.M., I have had an Indian garden of my own, and grow Navajo corn — blue, red, yellow, white and speckled– as well as other Indian vegetables which I use in my cooking. These I serve along with mutton, the most relished of meats by the Navajos.

"Kneel Down bread is so called because it is tied in a manner that makes the filled husks look as though they are kneeling."

6 fresh ears of corn
6 fresh corn husks
Salt to taste
Lard
Water

Cut kernels from cob, reserving the husks. Grind the kernels. By feel, add enough lard and water to the corn to make a paste. Fill the husks with this mixture and tie at both ends with string. Bend a third of the stuffed husks and tie again. Wrap in aluminum foil and bake at 350° for approximately an hour, or until firm to the touch. Kneel Down bread can also be baked directly on hot coals in a pit.

DOUGLAS JOHNSON

Photo – Ken Shar

Weewish or Luiseno

(Southern California Mission Indian Mush)

1. Find a Weewish tree (Southern California black oak).
2. Gather acorns.
3. Shell and dry acorn meats in the sun.
4. Chop, then grind on a metate.
5. Place ground acorns on flour sack cloth stretched over wooden grocery box.
6. Leach by pouring water over the ground acorns for several hours. This washes away tannic acid.
7. Now Weewish is ready to cook. The common way is to boil it and eat it like oatmeal. However, for the ultimate taste sensation, after boiling, let mush cool and jell. Then cut it in slices, put it in a pan with fat and fry it.
8. Fried acorn mush should be eaten out-of-doors with fry bread, jerky and strawberry soda pop.

FRITZ SCHOLDER

BETTINA STEINKE

Beer Muffins

3 cups Bisquick
3 teaspoons sugar
1 can beer

Grease muffin tins. Combine all ingredients and stir until blended. Pour into muffin tins and bake at 350° until brown and firm.

Makes 12 muffins.

"Being a career woman who works every day in the studio, I have had to learn to be a short order cook. This type of cooking can be very discouraging unless you develop the feeling that it is a dire necessity to inculcate inspiration into that brief evening hour, and to realize the important role which food plays in rounding out the day.

"I cannot take credit for this recipe; my husband brought it home from a boat captain in Galveston."

Photo – Jack & Betty Cheetham

ELMER W. SCHOOLEY

White Bread

2 packages dry yeast
1 teaspoon sugar
1/2 cup warm water

2 cups hot water
2 cups milk
2 tablespoons salt
1/3 cup sugar
6 tablespoons vegetable oil (peanut oil)
12 cups white flour

Prehumidify the oven with a large pan of water. Mix 2 packages of dry yeast with 1 teaspoon of sugar in 1/2 cup warm water. Put this in oven to start yeast growth.

Warm a large pan with hot water, empty, and put in 2 cups of hot water and 2 cups of milk. Add 2 tablespoons of salt and 1/3 cup of sugar. Add 6 tablespoons vegetable oil (we use peanut oil) and stir. Put this on a low heat burner so that the mixture stays comfortably warm to the finger. Stir in the yeast from the oven and when this is well mixed, stir in 12 cups of white flour. The last 2 cups should be added slowly, since the amount needed can vary. It may be mixed with a spoon, or, in the latter stages, with the hand. You have the right amount of flour when your floured hand does not stick to the dough.

Place in prewarmed oven for about an hour or until the mass has just about doubled. Grease pans. Divide risen dough into 4 equal parts. Knead and punch the dough. Shape and place in oiled pan, turn it over a couple of times so that the whole surface is oiled.

Put the loaves back in the oven until their size has doubled. Then remove water pan and bread. Preheat oven to 400°. Return to oven. Bake bread for 45 minutes.

Turn bread out of pans, cut off heel, butter and see how soon you can stop eating.

"My interest in cooking starts at the table and stops just before the dishes return to the kitchen. In between those events the blood runs hot, and perhaps hottest for bread. Fortunately my wife, the painter Gussie Dujardin, is as good a cook and baker as she is a painter, so we do little quarreling over recipes. I talked her into teaching me how to make bread. So this is really the Gussie Dujardin-Elmer W. Schooley Bread Recipe. But I still call her 'Master'."

ROGER d. SCHULTZ

Eggnog (an approach to)

I usually start with two eggs and put them in my "Dual Range 8" Osterizer (I've been known to use as many as four eggs). Then I press one of the following buttons: STIR/MIX, PUREE/CHOP, WHIP/BLEND, or GRATE/LIQUIFY; then I shove the red button into LO or HI and beat hell out of the eggs. (For added excitement I sometimes make the selection while not looking at the buttons which gives you 1 to 8 odds of hitting LIQUIFY and getting eggs all over the kitchen.)

The last time I made eggnog the second ingredient used was milk, but in looking back on the experience, I think that was perhaps the wrong thing to have done. . . (2 cups, for reference only.)

If I ever make eggnog again I'm going to make ice cream the second ingredient, and then add the necessary amount of milk to make the approximate total of eggnog I desire.

At least two giant serving spoonfuls of ice cream should be used; the flavor is often vanilla; however, that is not a hard and fast rule. For instance, I've always regarded black walnut flavor as a real taste treat.

The next procedure is to once again select and push the buttons of your choice. I like to get a good head of foam on the eggnog during this whirl, as it increases the pleasure of adding the remaining ingredients.

Next comes the salt, two shakes. (Notice the sound and sight of bursting foam bubbles.) Then sugar, four tablespoons plus or minus. Then comes another fun part, vanilla, four drops (watch it roar around and nearly make waves). Then two shakes of cinnamon, and then the final gourmet touch of six cranks of fresh ground nutmeg.

Once again I select and push buttons and give the eggnog its all-important final whirl.

DONALD B. ANDERSON

Sangrita

1 cup tomato juice
2 jiggers fresh orange juice
1 jigger fresh lime juice
Worcestershire sauce
Tabasco sauce
Allspice
Finely chopped onion
Salt
Pepper

Serve chilled, to accompany tequila as a chaser.

Photo – Joseph Anderson

ANN MOUL

Calavasas - New Mexico Style

Squash — A combination of zucchini, crookneck, summer squash, and Indian squash as available. Squashes are cut in 1-inch pieces.
2 cloves garlic, chopped
3 tomatoes, quartered
Several ears of corn, broken in pieces
Cilantro (also known as culantro, coriander, Chinese parsley) Use fresh cilantro, several sprigs chopped
1 fresh green chili, chopped
About 3 cups goat's milk, fresh or canned
Goat's cheese (crumbled) or ricotta
Salt
Mint (several fresh sprigs or dried to taste)

Sauté onion and garlic in olive oil or butter. Add chili and sauté one minute longer. Add squash, tomatoes, cilantro, mint; sauté several minutes. Add goat's milk, cover, cook 20 minutes. Add corn; cook 5 minutes longer. Salt to taste; sprinkle with goat's cheese. Turn off heat and let sit 20 minutes. The flavor really improves after sitting.

This is a New Mexican dish but interestingly it is similar to an ancient Peruvian dish, Chupe, a fantastic soup that contains milk, corn, cilantro, onions, garlic, tomatoes, chili (aji, a small hot red chili), potatoes, camarones (a fresh water crayfish) and fish. It is also similar to Colache, a Mexican dish that dates back to Aztec times.

Calavasas is a delicious, delightful and sensuous dish.

Photo — J.B. Smith

JIM HARRILL

Photo – Roger Beauchamp

Greek Lemon Soup

2 cans clear chicken broth (13-ounce can)
1 lemon
1 egg
1/2 teaspoon salt
1 cup precooked rice

    Heat 2 cans of clear chicken broth to boiling. Remove from heat. Add salt. Add juice from 1/2 lemon. Stir. Add 1 well-beaten egg to broth while stirring vigorously. Add one cup precooked rice. Return to heat, stirring moderately. Heat just to the boiling point. (If soup boils, egg will curdle.) Serve in bowl or cup with a thin slice of lemon.

    Serves 4.

    (Thin slices of chicken may be added with the rice for extra dividends.)

KRIS HOTVEDT

Black Walnut Shrimp Soup

"This, as well as other soups, can be served throughout the year; however, it is a summer favorite of mine. I serve it along with a large tossed salad, hot French bread and a dessert of fruit and cheese."

1 can creamed corn
1 pound cooked shrimp
1 cup sliced fresh mushrooms
2 green peppers, chopped
1/2 cup chopped onion
2 2-ounce packages black walnuts
Butter
1/2 gallon milk
Salt, pepper, sage

Sauté mushrooms, green peppers, onion and walnuts in butter. Mix the corn, shrimp and milk. Add all ingredients and heat to a simmer, cooking for about 10 or 15 minutes. Make 4 or 5 hours before serving. Refrigerate and heat before serving.

Photo – Herbert Lotz

JOSEPH A. CHAVEZ

Lantejas Con Chicharrones
(Lentil Soup)

1 cup lentils
1 cup chicharrones*
Salt to taste
1/2 small onion
1 teaspoon oregano
1/2 cup diced New Mexico green chili
Garlic
Water

Boil lentils in plenty of water for about 1 hour. Add salt and oregano, sautéed diced onion, sautéed chicharrones (chicharrones sauté in their own fat) and green chili with garlic. Simmer for about 1/2 hour, adding water as needed for a nice thick soup. Serve with sopaipillas.

Serves about 6.

*Chicharrones are a fried inner layer of pork skin having both fat and meat to it, and cut into delicate little squares. Not too many stores carry chicharrones. You will need to borrow some from a native New Mexican (Indian or Spanish probably). If you don't find any (chicharrones, not native New Mexicans) substitute 1 cup crisp-fried bacon chips.

MEGAN LLOYD HILL

Seafood Chowder

"My cooking career is characterized largely by its concessions. Lack of time and limited capacity for statistical calculation constitute a major indulgence in artistic license in my kitchen."

"Expandable quantities and flexible cooking time are cardinal rules. The most sympathetic exponent of this vagueness is Alice Brock, from whom this recipe originally came."

Milk
1 stick butter
1/4 pound bacon
Equal amounts of diced onion and potatoes
Any amount or combination of frozen, fresh or canned seafood. Oysters, clams, and frozen shrimp are suitable.
Paprika
Salt and pepper to taste

Place in large pot butter, diced bacon, potatoes, onions and paprika, and sauté until cooked through.

Add seafood and milk to desired thickness. When serving, add 1 tablespoon sherry to each individual bowl. Serve with buttered rolls and a dry white wine.

Serves 6.

Photo – Robert Nugent

CONSTANCE COUNTER

Multiple Choice Minestrone

3 medium-sized zucchini
1 large sweet red pepper
2 large celery stalks
1 green bell pepper
2 large onions
3 carrots, with skins on
1 cup cooked, small shell macaroni
1/2 cup cooked spaghetti
1 can tomato paste
1 large fresh tomato
4 large cloves garlic
1 1/2 pounds shank of beef, sliced through by the butcher
Salt and pepper to taste
2 teaspoons sweet basil
2 teaspoons oregano
1/2 cup hearty red wine
2 tablespoons olive oil
Water

Sauté meat, onions and garlic until browned. Add water and simmer for three hours, covered. Add vegetables, chopped, and other herbs. Cook until done. Add pasta, 1/2 cup wine, and tomato paste. Add more water as needed. Serve hot with tons of Parmesan cheese floated on the soup. Serve with French bread and Burgundy to good friends, who hopefully will enjoy it and engage in good conversation over dinner.

Optional ingredients: Mushrooms, parsley, navy beans, broccoli, other pastas. Just about any combination of vegetables and pasta can make an excellent minestrone.

"Homemade soup must be one of the better things in life."

Photo – J.B. Smith

ROBERT EWING

Consome De Pollo En Estilo Mexicano (Chicken soup, Mexican style)

FOR THE SOUP:
    1 whole small frying chicken (for 6 to 8 servings) *or* several chicken breasts (2 chicken breasts for 2 to 4 servings)
    1 small onion
    2 carrots
    Leaf oregano (as opposed to powdered)
    1 teaspoon sugar, or less
    Chicken consommé (granules rather than cubes)
    Salt and pepper

THE VEGETABLES:
    Fresh parsley
    Green onions
    Avocado
    Cherry tomatoes
    Small can chopped green chili
    Leaf oregano
    Limes

The amounts vary with the number of persons to be served.

Cover the chicken (or chicken breasts) with enough water to fill as many bowls as you will be serving and a little more for evaporation. Add the onion, chopped, and the carrot, scraped and cut in chunks. Add chicken consommé (I always bring back a healthy supply from the supermarket in Juarez when I visit Mexico, but the local product works as well) according to the amount of water. A small amount of sugar and a healthy pinch of oregano complete the brew. Simmer until the chicken is tender (about 45 minutes) and you should have a good rich chicken soup. Take the chicken out and let it cool while you chop up the vegetables. Pour hot water in *large* soup bowls and let them warm up while you wash and chop the parsley, wash and chop the green onions, peel and chop (large chops) the avocado, wash and halve or quarter the cherry tomatoes, skin the chicken and cut into small pieces and open the can of green chili.

Empty the hot water from the bowls and to each one add about a tablespoon of chopped parsley, a teaspoon of chopped onion, as much avocado as you can afford and about as many tomatoes as you wish. Green chili should be added according to your guests' tolerance for same, from a teaspoon to a tablespoon, and add a lot of cut up chicken. A pinch of leaf oregano and you are ready to add the strained soup (about two cups per serving) as boiling hot as you can make it. Your guests should be seated and poised for eating since the vegetables cool the soup quickly and it's best *very* hot with the vegetables still crisp. Also have a small bowl ready with quartered limes and let each person squeeze in lime juice as the last touch.

I serve the soup with *nachos* (a purely Texan invention) — easily made by quartering corn tortillas and topping each quarter with a dab of refried beans (canned are fine), a bit of chopped green chili, a hunk of longhorn cheese and a sprinkle of oregano and put under the broiler until the cheese melts.

A fruit dessert seems to be the best complement for the meal which is really soup, salad and main dish in one.

Buen provecho!

Photo – Herbert Lotz

Vegetable Soup and Party Pintos

PETER HURD

Peter Hurd is known for his paintings of the Southwest. From a culinary standpoint, his fame is more obscure. Hurd favors a home-on-wheels from which he can paint, travel back roads and generally do his thinking and creating. His camper bus contains all the niceties of a house: stove, refrigerator, bed, table, shower, etc. His favorite recipe is:

Take one small saucepan, fill with water from the pump, bring to a boil and add one package of Lipton's vegetable beef soup. Bring to a boil a second time, and serve in tin cup with several-day-old bread.

The following recipe is for special occasions and has been served to a rather large segment of people in WHO'S WHO:

        1 can pinto beans
        1 can chopped green chile

Open can of pintos. Place in pan. Open can of chili, add to pan. Stir with tongue depressor till hot. Serve outdoors on paper plates. Embellish with edible roadside greens if occasion demands. Not exactly cordon blue, but very tasty after a hundred miles of ranch roads.

Photo – Ken Cobean

CHUZO TAMOTZU

This is a variation of a traditional Japanese recipe. Tsukumono is to the Japanese what chutney is to those of India, an accompaniment to the main dish. It is always served in small dishes to enhance meat or fish.

Tsukumono Slice a cucumber paper thin, slantwise. Toss with salt to taste and 1/2 teaspoon of brown sugar. Add 1/4 cup apple cider vinegar and let stand ten minutes or so. Sprinkle crushed nori (seaweed) and sesame seed over top. One dish of tsukumono per person.

Photo – Holly Beckley

MIRIAM & SEYMOUR TUBIS

Russian Borscht

This is a typical borscht from the region of the Ukraine. Both Tubises' families are from this area—Miriam's maternal grandparents from Zhitomir and Seymour's from Nosovka, near Kiev.

1 medium head cabbage, shredded
1 large can tomatoes
1 whole onion
1 pound soup meat (beef) and one or two marrow bones
2 tablespoons brown sugar
Juice of one lemon
1 cup beef bouillon
1/2 cup shredded celery leaves
Salt and pepper
1 medium can julienne beets, plus juice

Simmer all the above ingredients for at least two hours — the longer the better, adding more bouillon or water as it cooks, plus juice from one medium can of julienne beets. Toward the end of the cooking time, add the beets. Taste for seasoning, adding more sugar, lemon juice, salt and pepper if necessary. The borscht should be slightly tart, slightly sweet. Remove bones, onions and meat. Cube meat and return it to pot. Serve in large bowls with dollops of sour cream.

CLIFF HARMON

Turnip Inspiration

1/3 cup sliced almonds or Brazil nuts
1 large turnip, coarsely grated
1 large potato, coarsely grated
2 heaping tablespoons chopped fresh parsley
1 chopped green onion
1 teaspoon oil

In a large heavy frying pan or Chinese wok, sauté nuts in oil over moderate heat for 10 minutes or until slightly browned. Distribute the nuts evenly over pan. Mix vegetables well and add to nuts. Cover and continue cooking over a moderate fire until potatoes brown, about 20 minutes. Turn carefully with a spatula and finish cooking. Serves 4.

"This is my own recipe and is in constant use in season."

HAROLD FORE

Photo – Bart – Durham Lab., Inc.

Harry's Beans

"A recent San Francisco tradition, transported to and transmogrified by the sanguine and delicate gastronomical practices of the mid-Southwest.

"When I was younger, I made a vow, probably shared by millions, that when I grew up I would buy and eat anything, or combination of things, that my heart, mind or stomach desired. This particular meal meets all my prerequisites and has proved easy to live with through many years, rich and poor."

2 large cans pork and beans (the cheaper, the better)
1/4 pound grated cheddar cheese
1 Spanish onion, grated
1/4 cup blackstrap molasses
1/4 pound butter
Garlic to taste
1/2 cup brown sugar
1/2 pound bacon
1/2 package chopped smoky link sausage
Dash of Tabasco sauce
Salt and pepper to taste

Take all ingredients except the bacon and combine in a large iron pot. Cook this over a low heat for about 45 minutes. Fry bacon crisp and crumble it in just before serving with toasted, buttered English muffins.

I'm very glad to share this meal with all of you.

Zucchini Ginger Custard

This custard is an excellent main dish for a vegetarian dinner or can be served with meat, fish or fowl with equal success.

1 tablespoon oil (olive, peanut, or safflower)
3 or 4 medium-sized zucchini, thinly sliced
1/2 cup diced onion, white or green
1 teaspoon salt
2 cups milk
2 teaspoons grated fresh ginger or 1/2 teaspoon powdered ginger (or to taste)
4 eggs, well-beaten

Heat oil in frying pan over medium heat. Add squash and onion, stirring until onion is translucent. Transfer to a small shallow baking dish holding about 5 or 6 cups.

In a small saucepan mix milk, salt and ginger. Heat until small bubbles form around rim. Stir occasionally. Slowly blend hot milk mixture into beaten egg. Pour over squash-onion mix. Set baking pan in dish of hot water in oven. Bake at 350° until set, about 35 minutes. Serve immediately.

Makes about 4 servings.

SAM SCOTT

SWAZO

Squaw Corn

1/2 pound bacon
1 3/4 cups canned cream style corn
2 eggs, beaten
Salt and pepper to taste

Dice bacon and fry in skillet until crisp. Pour off all but 2 tablespoons fat and add corn and eggs. Season. Cook over low heat, stirring until eggs are creamy and thickened.

Serves 4.

French Fried Onion Rings

1 large Spanish onion
2/3 cup milk
1/2 cup flour (if using self-rising flour, omit baking powder and salt)
3/4 teaspoon baking powder
1/4 teaspoon salt
Fat or oil

Peel onion, cut into 1/4 inch slices and separate into rings. Heat fat or oil (1 inch deep) to 375° in large skillet. Beat remaining ingredients with rotary beater until smooth. Dip each onion ring into batter, letting excess drip into bowl. Fry a few onion rings at a time in hot fat about 2 minutes or until golden brown, turning once. Drain.

Serves 3 or 4.

JOHN PHILIP WAGNER

Tree of Life Salad
(10,000 Year Old Recipe)

Rub 1 large prehistoric bowl with garlic.
Place in it 2 handfuls of raw Yucca Baccata fruit, chopped and seeded;
one handful of dandelion greens; one handful of Magic Mushrooms.
Peel, slice and add:
one hard-boiled pterodactyl egg.
Toss the salad in 1/3 cup of crushed corn juice.

Serve at once.

Photo – Siegfried Halus

HELEN HARDIN

Photo – Al Cabral

Green Chili Omelette

"When I was first living off my paintings, eggs were cheap and nutritious. Eggs, however, can become quite boring, so by adding what happens to be my favorite food, green chili, I managed to get through hard times and stay fairly healthy."

6 large eggs
1/2 cup sour cream
1/2 teaspoon MSG
Salt, if desired
8 ounces grated cheese. (I like to use mild cheddar or muenster; or, for a real treat, try cream cheese.)

Sauce:
1 cup green chili, chopped
4 large fresh tomatoes, quartered
1/2 cup onion, chopped
1/2 teaspoon crushed garlic
Salt to taste
Olive oil

Prepare sauce first: Fry onions in olive oil until clear; add tomatoes, fry for a minute, then add chili. You may add 1/2 cup water and the salt and garlic, cover, turn heat very low to simmer.

Eggs: This may surprise some people, but I like to prepare the eggs in the blender. I think this comes from using sour cream, and it does make the omelette lighter. Blend the eggs, sour cream, MSG and salt. Then pour in a large skillet, using olive oil or butter on the bottom to keep from sticking. Cook on very low heat with a cover, until the top of the mixture has set.

Then put the cheese on the top, covering one half of the omelette, and fold the other half covering the cheese.

Now, cut in half and put on a warm plate; cover with sauce.

Eat well!

Serves 2 starving artists.

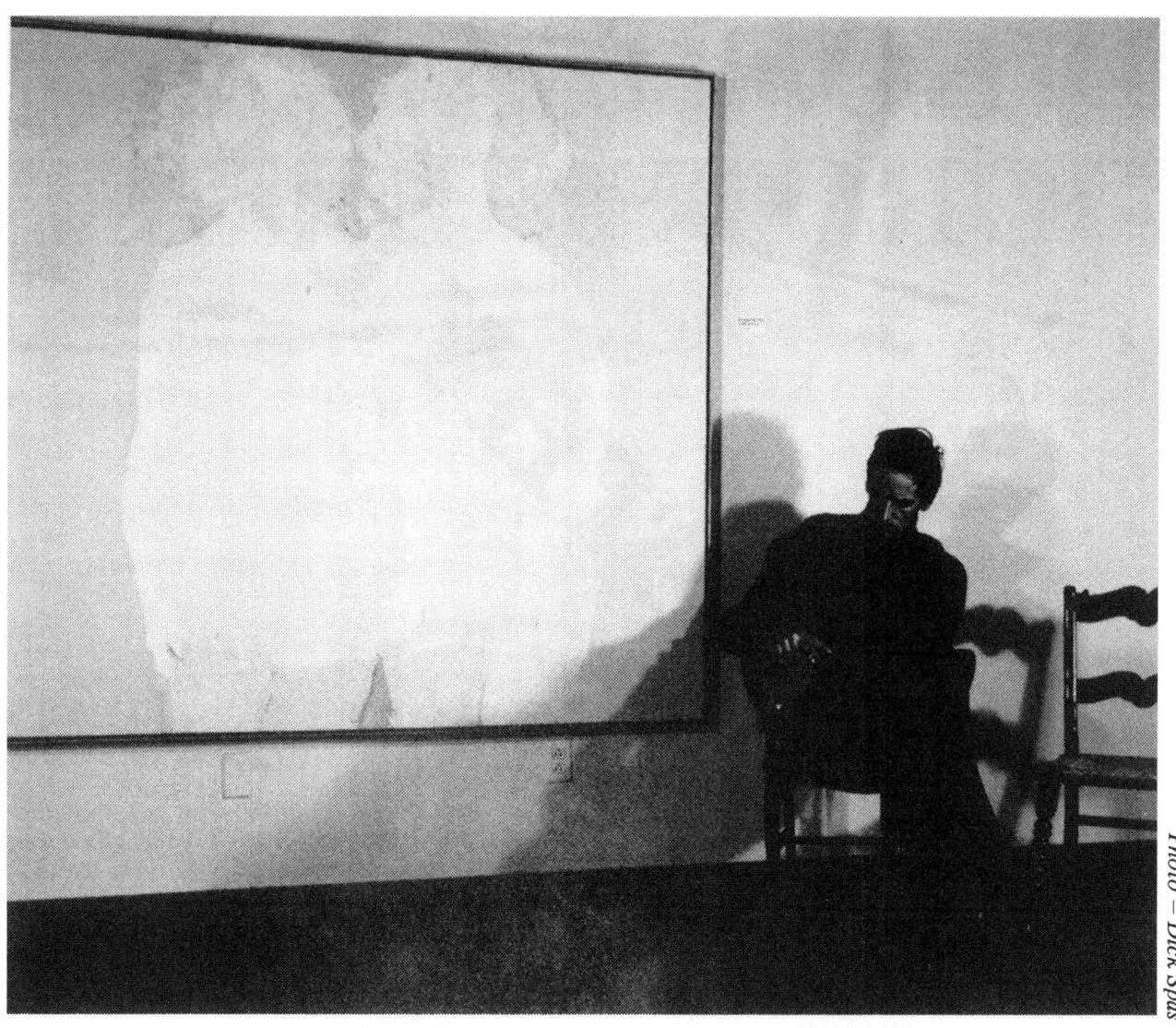

Photo – Dick Spas

Liver, Omelette, Cabbage Dinner

1 pound calf liver
1/2 large head of red cabbage
Some red cooking wine
1/2 to 1 cup tomato sauce
4 large fresh eggs
1 cup loosely grated cheddar cheese
Salt and pepper to taste

Skin and fillet the liver. Shake it in a bag of whole wheat flour or cornmeal. Cook the liver quickly in a covered, oiled frying pan until done.

Slice the cabbage across into 1/8 inch slices. Sauté the cabbage first in cooking oil. Make a broth with the tomato sauce and cooking wine. Simmer the cabbage in this liquid until cabbage has lost its toughness.

Whip up the eggs. Stir in the cheese. Cook omelette until fluffy, add cheddar cheese and fold. Sprinkle fresh parsley over the omelette and serve.

WESLEY RUSNELL

"Good food, good cooking, can increase the vivid values in one's life. The life of a family can flower up from the roots of this domestic art. Isn't it, after all, perhaps a form of love?"

A side dish of yogurt goes well with the cabbage, creating a kind of sweet-sour byplay.

Serves 2-3.

HONORABLE DOROTHY BRETT

Photo – Terrence Moore

Eggs a la Brett

Boil water. Simply drop egg in, cook.
Serve with an English muffin and, of course,
Oxford marmalade. "It's the best, you know."

Drink with champagne, if you've got it!

Serves 1.

NICK ABDALLA

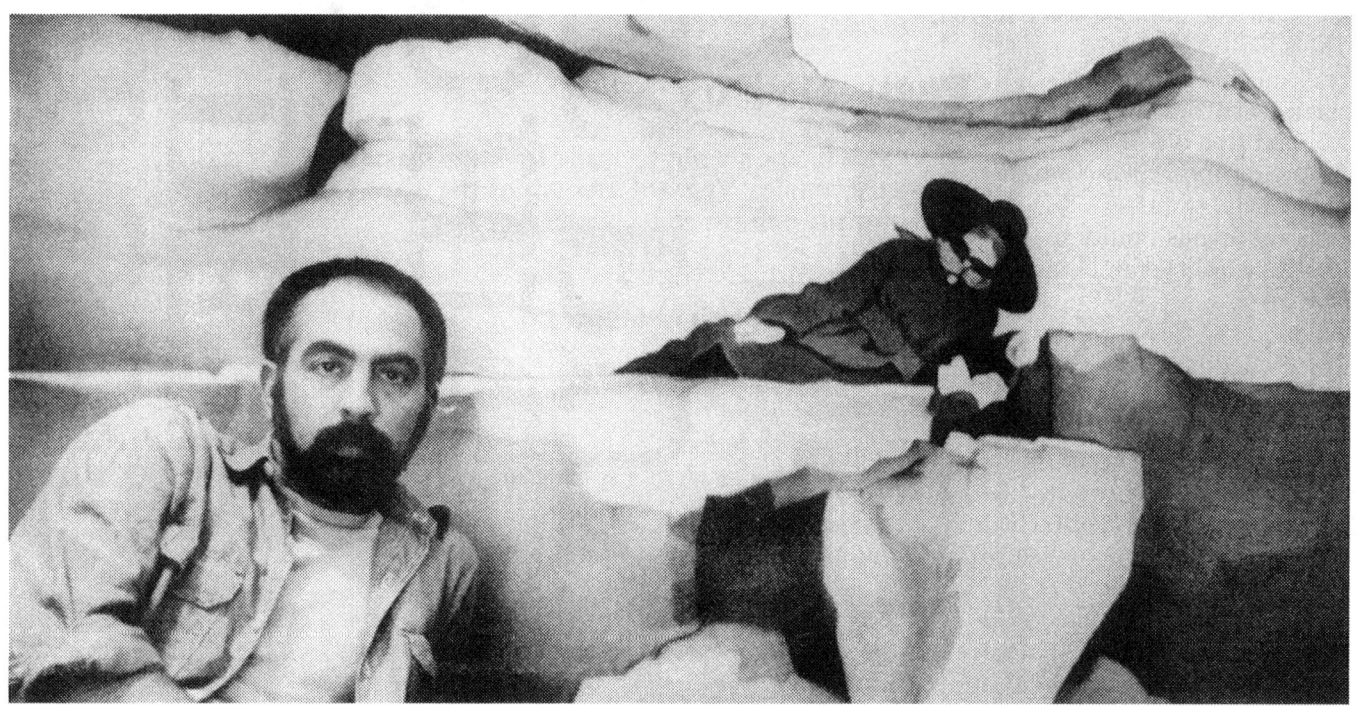

Bearnaise Sauce

Wonderful for red, juicy meats; especially good for fondue! Equally superb on French bread, poached or boiled eggs.

1/2 cup dry white wine
2 tablespoons tarragon vinegar
1 tablespoon finely chopped chervil
2 crushed peppercorns
1 sprig parsley or 1 tablespoon snipped parsley
1 tablespoon finely chopped green onions

Combine above ingredients; bring to boil over direct heat. Boil until ingredients are half their original volume. Remove from heat.

Place mixture in a double boiler. Add gradually:

  3 egg yolks
  1 cup melted butter

Using a wire whisk to stir, add small amounts of egg, then butter, alternating and constantly stirring until the mixture thickens. Allow to cool to room temperature, and serve. IT IS IMPORTANT TO USE ONLY SMALL AMOUNTS OF EGG AND BUTTER, AND TO BEAT CONSTANTLY, TO AVOID CURDLING.

JOHN DE PUY

Pasta De Puy

"This recipe should be made for large masses of hungry people. Vary the amount of the ingredients for the number to be served."

Fresh mushrooms
Italian tomatoes (fresh or canned)
Chopped ripe olives
Whole oregano leaves, to taste
Fresh garlic, to taste
Chopped Spanish onions
Roasted whole green chilis (or canned)
Olive oil
Sherry
Grated cheddar cheese
Egg noodles

Sauté in frying pan (nothing else will do) garlic, onions, mushrooms. Add all other ingredients, except green chili, cheddar cheese and noodles. Simmer uncovered for approximately 1 hour.

Cook egg noodles. Grease casserole. Place noodles in casserole and add sauce. Cut chili in strips, place on sauce, cover with cheddar cheese. Place in 350° oven until heated through.

Photo – Terrence Moore

DENNIS LARKINS

Photo – Cradoc L. Bagshaw

Gregarious Goulash

1 pound ground beef
2-3 cloves garlic, chopped
1/2 large onion, chopped
1/2 bell pepper, chopped
1 large can tomatoes or 3 fresh tomatoes
1 small can tomato paste
12 ounces elbow macaroni
1 teaspoon oregano
2 bay leaves
1 teaspoon dried parsley
Salt and pepper to taste

Optional:
Mushrooms, corn, peas, green onions, dried red chili, thyme

Serves 4 to 6.

Brown in large frying pan the hamburger, garlic and chopped onions plus herbs and seasoning. Add tomatoes, paste, bell pepper and enough water to almost fill pan. Add optional ingredients at this time. Add macaroni. Bring to full boil, reduce to medium heat and continue boiling lightly, stirring occasionally until macaroni is fully cooked. After approximately 20-30 minutes, the water will have boiled down to a thick sauce. Additional water and seasoning may be necessary.

CHARLOTTE B. BRUCE

Spicy-Kraut Casserole

1 pound ground beef
1 egg
1/2 teaspoon salt
1/4 teaspoon black pepper
1/3 cup chopped onion
1/2 cup bread crumbs, preferably whole wheat
1 tablespoon oil
1 16-ounce can of sauerkraut (save juice)
1 tablespoon vinegar
1/2 teaspoon ground ginger
1/2 cup tomato juice
1/2 cup beer
1 tablespoon cornstarch
1/4 cup brown sugar
1/4 cup seedless raisins
1 apple, cored and chopped

Mix meat with egg, bread crumbs, salt, pepper and onion. Shape in one-inch balls; cook in oil until just cooked through. Place in shallow 1 1/2 quart casserole. Set aside.

Keep 1 tablespoon of oil in skillet. Mix cornstarch with vinegar, juice from sauerkraut, tomato juice and beer and ginger. Heat in skillet until thickened. Arrange sauerkraut around meat balls and pour sauce over all. Top with combined sugar, raisins, and chopped apple. Bake at 300-325°, about 20 minutes, or until hot and bubbly. Good, and inexpensive!

JIM WOOD

Photo — Duncan Mac Innes

Eggplant Casserole

1/3 cup olive oil
3/4 cup onions, chopped
2 garlic cloves, chopped
4 green bell peppers, sliced
2 1/2 cups eggplant, peeled and diced
3 cups zucchini, diced
2 cups tomatoes, peeled and quartered

In deep skillet or heavy casserole, put olive oil.

Sauté until golden — onion and garlic cloves.

Add green bell peppers, eggplant, zucchini and tomatoes.

Simmer covered over low heat for 35-45 minutes. Uncover for 10 minutes more to reduce liquid. Serve and eat.

"I don't know much about cooking, but I know what I like."

BERNIQUE LONGLEY

Chicken Liver Pâté

1 pound chicken livers
2 hard-cooked eggs
1/2 cup parsley, chopped
1/2 cup celery, in coarse chunks
1/3 cup onion, coarsely chopped
2/3 to 1 cup mayonnaise
Fresh ground black pepper
1/2 to 1 teaspoon salt
1/4 teaspoon curry powder
1/2 teaspoon Beau Monde seasoning
1/2 clove garlic
Flour

Dredge chicken livers in flour and sauté in butter until browned. To livers, add all remaining ingredients except mayonnaise and chop on board with cleaver. Put mayonnaise atop ingredients to be chopped. The mayonnaise keeps mixture in place. If you do not wish to chop by hand, use food grinder and add mayonnaise to chopped mixture.

Chill before serving. Make a mound of the pâté on a platter, sprinkle with chopped parsley and surround with saltine crackers or buffet rye bread.

Additions can be made, such as olives (black or ripe), piñon nuts, etc., to alter the recipe.

HENRIETTE WYETH

Chicken Sentinela

2 chickens (disjointed)
1 cup chopped green chili, peeled,
 or 1 cup mushrooms
1 pint heavy cream
3 cans cream of chicken soup
Oregano
Savor salt
Salt

Place disjointed pieces of chicken in well-buttered baking dish. Make sauce of cream, chopped green chili, cream of chicken soup. Season to taste. Pour sauce over chicken and bake one hour at 375°. Serve with crisp green salad and hot homemade bread. Serves 6.

Henriette Wyeth, Mrs. Peter Hurd, is a dual artist—easel and kitchen. The favored people who have had the privilege of dinner at her table have carried her fame to far corners. The Hurd ranch is named Sentinel, hence Chicken Sentinela.

Photo – Ken Cobean

BARBARA VOM LEHN

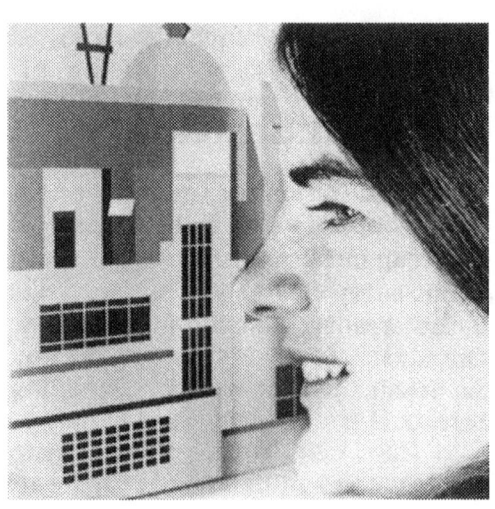

Arroz Con Pollo (Rice with chicken)

Arroz con pollo is considered a festive dish in both Mexico and the Dominican Republic, where I have lived — and cooked. Chicken is an expensive item in both countries, unlike the United States where it is the most economical fare to buy. It can be ordered in any restaurant, from the lowliest to the most luxurious, and is invariably delicious and satisfying to all. Here it can be served with equal success to either a troop of hungry children or a mob of ravenous artists. It would be very *tipico* served on a platter garnished with *tostones* — slices of plantain. These are green bananas that are fried, mashed flat, and refried, a crisp challenge to the softer chicken mixture.

1 chicken, cut up
1/2 cup olive oil
Salt, cayenne pepper to taste

Sprinkle the chicken liberally with salt and cayenne pepper. Brown in hot olive oil. Remove to platter.

1 1/2 cups rice
1 medium-sized onion, chopped
6 cloves garlic, chopped
1 green pepper, finely chopped

In the same pan the chicken was browned in, sauté the rice and vegetables until the grains of rice are milky white.

2 cups boiling water
2 tablespoons tomato paste
1 tablespoon chicken stock powder, or 3 chicken bouillon cubes
Dash of cumin
Dash of saffron
Salt to taste

While the rice is sautéeing, combine the liquid ingredients. When the rice is ready, return the chicken to the pan and pour the liquid mixture over the top. Cover the pan with a tight-fitting lid and turn the heat down as low as possible. When the rice has absorbed the liquid, but is yet in separate grains, the dish is ready to serve. A small can of chopped black olives can be added for additional color and interest.

Serves 6.

JANET LIPPINCOTT

Long Island Duckling

" As a young child and later as an adolescent, I remember well the train ride to the far end of Long Island for a visit to my grandmother's. About halfway there, the train passed the Long Island Duck Farmers, where a sea captain in 1873 brought the first white Peking ducks around the Horn. As I glanced out of the window, there seemed to be thousands of them, either sunning themselves or swimming in a small pond.

"Now, here in the West, one frequently comes across a frozen, ready-to-cook, packaged Long Island Duckling of around five pounds. Here is my favorite way to cook a duck for no more than four people."

Preheat the oven to 325⁰. Wash the duck under cold running water and put the giblets aside. With salt and pepper rub the inside and outside and skewer neck skin to the back of the duckling. (One can also sprinkle a good quality soy sauce.) Any suitable prepared dressing with two tablespoons of butter and one sliced onion will do for stuffing. Place on rack in a roasting pan; do not add water or cover. After 2½ hours the skin will be crisp and golden brown. When a leg moves freely it is done and there should be no fat under the skin. (Remember from time to time to prick with a fork to let the fat escape.) Giblets may be simmered in salted water for gravy.

"I want to say also that a duckling can be served with a rice stuffing, a red cabbage stuffing or a sauerkraut and apple stuffing. As for sauces, an orange or spicy cranberry sauce is not to be overlooked. A vegetable to be seved with this succulent bird is peeled white turnips cut in two-inch-long olive shapes. Divine."

FORD RUTHLING

New Mexico Ranch Pan Fried Steak
(A regional adaptation of Ranch Pan-Fried steak, an adaptation of fried steak)

Any beef steak
Salt
Pepper
Bacon rind
Roasted and peeled green chili, preferably from Velarde, N.M.

Preheat seasoned black skillet to 380°. Rub bacon rind around inside bottom of skillet, sprinkle salt and pepper liberally into bottom of pan.

Fry steak on one side, turn over, cover steak with plenty of green chili. Serve hot. If steak is tough and flavorless, garnish with Sauce Ruthling, which is lots of catsup.

"There is no excuse for a bad meal. I find that the best meals laid upon my table have been prepared by my unsuspecting friends who have dropped by casually and been commandeered to kitchen duties while I painted."

Photo – Herbert Lotz

WILLIAM LUMPKINS

Photo – Richard Smith

Chuck Wagon Ranch Steak

From your butcher, secure one-pound round steaks (one per person), top round, rump or shoulder, whichever is the cheapest that day.

Mix a seasoning flour using 4 cups of flour, 4 teaspoons salt, 1 teaspoon pepper and 1 teaspoon paprika. First brown the steak in hot fat. Mix seasoning flour with 2 cups of water, and pour over steaks. The best pan for this is a dutch oven, but if you don't have one, use a 5-inch deep pan with a tight cover.

Cover and simmer for 30 minutes. Slice whole red onions about 1/4 inch thick. At the end of the 30 minutes, open pan and place onions over meat at least two layers thick. Close pan and simmer for another hour. Serve with plenty of the gravy and onions, and you will know why the cowpokes always yelled with such gusto as they rode off into the sunset.

AGNES SIMS

Beef Stew

"Here is my favorite beef stew recipe, and all four of my dogs love it."

Shank of beef cut through in 2-inch pieces
    (or the amount of flank steak you will need, marinated in claret or burgundy)
Flour
Herbs to your liking
Dash paprika
3 tablespoons bacon drippings
1 large sliced onion
Salt and pepper to taste
1 can bouillon soup, undiluted
1 cup red wine (if flank was used, use wine from marinade)
Small whole peeled onions
Small peeled potatoes
Scraped small carrots
2 peeled tomatoes
1 stalk celery cut into bite-size pieces
2 small peeled turnips (if you like them)
If necessary, a few drops Kitchen Bouquet to darken
Brown sugar

Flour the meat and brown in an iron kettle or stew pan in the bacon drippings, along with the sliced onion. When the meat is brown on all sides, add salt and pepper, the bouillon and red wine. Simmer covered for 1 1/2 hours over low heat until meat is fairly tender. Add brown sugar, onions, carrots, potatoes, tomatoes, celery, turnips. Simmer until tender. Never use vegetables which have already been cooked.

If you like a thick gravy, add a roux of flour mixed with water. Add a dash of Worcestershire sauce or Kitchen Bouquet. Let sit for an hour or so, or overnight. (It improves the flavor.)

Remove excess grease and stir in a tablespoon of grated Parmesan or Romano cheese. Stir and let simmer for ten minutes.

Serve with hot buttered French bread and a tossed salad.

Photo – The Santa Fean

JOHN MEIGS

River House Roast

1 chuck roast, 2 to 3 pounds
1 can spinach
1 can kernel corn
2 minced onions
1 cup soy sauce
1/4 pound butter
1 can tomatoes, Italian style
2 cups fresh mushrooms
Salt to taste
Coarse ground pepper

Heat roasting pan to 400°. Remove from oven and place butter in pan and cover pan as it melts. Place roast in pan. Place on top of stove, sear for 5 minutes on one side, turn and sear the other side. Remove from heat and add soy sauce, minced onions, pepper, salt. Cover with spinach and corn; dot with butter. Bake covered in 300° oven for 1 1/2 hours.
Add tomatoes and mushrooms; cook 1/2 hour longer. Serve on hot plates garnished with fresh mint.

John Meigs is an artist-author, writing books about his neighbor Peter Hurd, and most recently, a book, *The Cowboy in American Prints*. He is also responsible for the decor and architecture of a series of restaurants which have become famous for steaks, trout and lobster.

Photo – Ken Cobean

ABU BAKR

Barbecued Goat's Ribs (Cabrito)

Preheat oven to 325°.

Parboil, in a large pot on top of stove, tender goat's ribs for approximately one hour.

Meanwhile, cover large cookie sheet with tin foil. Remove ribs from pot, pat dry, and lay them out on tin foil. Wet ribs thoroughly with white vinegar, then sprinkle liberally with garlic powder, salt and pepper, which should adhere well to the vinegar.

Now one is ready to drench the ribs in barbecue sauce:

Mix together:
   2 cups commercial barbecue sauce (I recommend Open Pit plain barbecue sauce)
   Juice of 2 freshly squeezed lemons
   1/2 cup catsup
   3 tablespoons white vinegar
   Several drops Louisiana hot sauce
   Dash of garlic powder

Pour about half of this tangy sauce over the ribs and bake slowly for one hour, then turn ribs over, pour more sauce on them and cook for another hour or so.

With remaining sauce poured on ribs, serve with buttered rice and your best tossed salad.

R.C. GORMAN

Baked Prairie Dog

The prairie dog is a great delicacy among the Navajos. March is the month to hunt these small animals.

Dress your prairie dog and salt immediately. Stuff with cooked wild rice or with diced potatoes, green chili, and onions. Sew up or secure with skewers. Wrap in aluminum foil and bake for 1½ hours at 350°. Serves 2. Serve with a vin rosé, well-chilled.

Photo – J.B. Smith

CYNTHIA BISSELL

Photo – J.B. Smith

Johann Sebastian Pork

1 loin of pork, 4-6 pounds
4 big onions
6 green cooking apples
2 cloves garlic
1 tablespoon ground sage
1 tablespoon ground ginger
1 or 2 cups red wine or apple cider
Salt and pepper to taste

Trim loin of pork of excess fat. Cut slits and place garlic slivers in them. Rub roast with sage and ginger. Place roast in hot oven, 400°, uncovered for 20 minutes to sear. Place sliced onions around roast, turn oven down to 300° and pour wine on roast, cover and roast about 1 hour per pound. An hour before roast is done, put quartered apples around roast, cover again until cooked. Serve with rice.

RICHARD MAITLAND

"Being a Scorpio (they usually think they can top anything), I have even tried to improve on traditional Indian cooking after having lived in India for five years. One of my many experiments resulted in the following recipe. This includes the primary ingredients of many dishes of the Parsi community, whose forefathers were of Persian descent."

Bombay Brinjal

2 large eggplants
1 pound ground lamb (or mutton)
1 cup cashew nuts
2 eggs
1 medium onion
1 clove garlic
1 large tomato
1 tablespoon curry powder
1 1/2 tablespoons fresh ground ginger root
1/2 teaspoon salt
1/2 cup yogurt

Halve eggplants and scrape out pulp. Steam pulp for 10 minutes and chop finely. Fry the meat, onions, garlic and seasonings lightly in butter. Do not overcook. When cool, mix in the crushed tomato, eggplant pulp, beaten eggs, ½ cup nuts, and yogurt. Fill eggplant shells with the mixture. Bake for approximately 45 minutes in 350° oven. Fry remaining nuts in butter and use for garnish on your Bombay Brinjal.

Serves 4.

Serve with a side dish of chilled cucumbers tossed in yogurt with chopped fresh mint and a little lime juice. And, of course, a hot-sweet mango chutney.

Photo – Hugh Weymouth

GLYNN

Christmas Fish Dip

2 large family-size cans light chunky tuna, well drained
6 hard-boiled eggs, well peeled and finely chopped
1/2 teaspoon wine vinegar
1 teaspoon Italian olive oil
1 whole onion, medium-sized (any color), finely diced
1 1/2 cups mayonnaise (homemade for better results)
1 cup currants
1 truffle, finely ground
2 Bombay duck, crumbled
2 to 4 firm but hot, light green, bottled chili peppers, seeded and finely minced
1 strong dash garlic oil, salt, or 1 finely mashed small garlic clove
4 teaspoons curry powder or less (to taste)
1/4 teaspoon cracked pepper
1 dash cayenne pepper
1/2 teaspoon salt
1 teaspoon sugar
1 dash paprika

Combine above ingredients excluding ground truffle, dash of paprika, Bombay duck.

Whip mixture into fine paste. Place on bed of lettuce. Chill in refrigerator 1/2 hour. Sprinkle excluded ingredients over top of dip.

"I have found that everything that I have prepared to date goes exceedingly well with hot dogs and champagne."

GOMEZ

Photo – Robert Nugent

HARRIETT M. SUTTON

Pork Chop and Bean Casserole

1 large can pork and beans
1/2 cup catsup
1/4 cup brown sugar
1/4 cup water
1 large onion
4 to 6 pork chops

Grease casserole.

Mix first four ingredients and put in casserole. Brown pork chops seperately. Place pork chops on top of beans, cover with sliced onion, salt and pepper. Bake at 350° 1 to 1 1/2 hours, depending on thickness of pork chops.

"I like quick recipes, or recipes that can be prepared in advance and then popped into the oven. Even with advance preparations I've been known to let that special casserole burn, having become so engrossed in my painting and losing all track of time."

Photo – Don Engdahl

CECIL HOWARD

Raisin Delicious

1 cup brown sugar, packed
1 1/2 cups boiling water
1 tablespoon butter
1/4 teaspoon cinnamon
1/4 teaspoon salt
1 cup raisins
1 teaspoon vanilla
2 tablespoons butter
1/3 cup sugar or honey
3/4 cups whole wheat flour
1 teaspoon baking powder
1/4 teaspoon salt
1/2 cup sweet milk
1/3 cup hulled sunflower seeds or coarsely chopped nut meats

Mix sugar, water, butter, cinnamon, salt and raisins in saucepan and boil to a medium syrup (about 15 minutes); remove from heat and add vanilla.

Meanwhile, prepare drop batter as follows: Cream butter and sugar until blended. Add to well-mixed dry ingredients and stir together. Pour in milk and stir until thoroughly blended. Place batter in well-greased 9-inch square baking pan and spoon the raisin syrup over it. Sprinkle with sunflower seeds or nuts and bake in moderate oven (350°) for about 30 minutes, or until golden brown. Serve warm or cold with cream or yogurt.

This recipe makes only 5 or 6 servings, so I usually double it, as we like this for breakfast as well as for dessert.

RINI PRICE

Peaches Lawrence
(or Strawberry Howard)

4 very large, ripe, peeled peaches; or 2 big boxes of strawberries (2 or 3 pints) — depending on the season
5 to 6 jiggers of white rum
6 to 10 tablespoons of sugar
1 pint whipping cream.

In a medium-sized bowl, slice the fruit into small pieces, sugaring them with what looks like too much sugar. Stir vigorously.

Add four jiggers of rum and stir again. Let the rum, fruit and sugar mixture steep as long as possible in the refrigerator — the longer the better. Then, just before serving, add some additional rum to spike the flavor, stir vigorously, and fill the bowl with the pint of whipping cream. The whipping cream should *not* be whipped. Stir again until cream bubbles slightly.

This is a fast, nourishing, very rich summertime desset that is best after souffles or omelettes. Very little work, but luxurious results.

JEAN PROMUTICO

Uncooked Russian Cheesecake (Pasha)

"This past winter I cooked and baked in a wood cookstove. Come the warm weather, I acquired an electric hotplate for cooking rather than suffer through a super-hot kitchen from having stoked the stove. This, of course, meant that I was left without an oven, and without homemande gookies for special days and company events. But instead of accepting this fact, I ferreted through a lot of books and found this very nutritious UNCOOKED cheesecake that is as wonderful as any baked one."

Beat with electric mixer until smooth:
    2 pounds hoop cheese, or dry unsalted cottage cheese
    ¼ pound sweet (unsalted) butter

Sift together: ¼ cup powdered milk
                1¼ cups sugar
Add to cheese and butter mixture.

Add and stir well:
    1 cup top milk or cream
    1 cup chopped, blanched almonds
    2 tablespoons vanilla or grated vanilla bean
    1/4 cup finely chopped candied fruit

Cover colander with clean cloth; pour cheese mixture over cloth and place a small inverted plate on top as weight. Set colander on cake pan and let stand in refrigerator overnight.

Turn cake onto large plate, remove cloth, slice, serve. Any leftover may be frozen.

Very rich — a little goes a long way.

MARGARET HERRERA CHAVEZ

Flan

1 1/4 cups sugar
3 tablespoons sugar
3 cups whole milk
5 medium eggs
1 cup water
Vanilla to taste
Butter
Pinch of salt

Using a small saucepan, caramelize 1 1/4 cups of sugar with 1 cup water. Set aside. In a double boiler place milk, remaining sugar, pinch of salt. Separate eggs and blend into flan mixture, adding vanilla. Bring to a gentle boil and turn off heat.

Place the caramel mixture in the bottom of a baking dish, pour in flan and set baking dish in a larger pan with water. Bake approximately 45 minutes or until the custard sets. Sprinkle with crushed nuts and serve hot or chilled.

Photo – Dick Berg

FORREST MOSES

Mother Moses' Ole Southern Chocolate Chess Pie

"This may very well be the best chocolate pie you have ever eaten."

2/3 stick butter
1 1/2 squares Baker's chocolate
1 1/4 cups sugar (half brown, half white)
2 large eggs
1 teaspoon Cointreau
1/2 cup evaporated milk

Melt butter with chocolate. Then add other ingredients. Blend mixture smooth, pour into 9-inch uncooked pie shell and bake for 30 or 40 minutes at 375°.

The pie will swell and puff up in the oven and then settle as it cools into a dense firm center.

Serve warn or cold. Add topping of whipped cream flavored with Cointreau (about ½ teaspoon) to taste and then spoon fresh blackberries or strawberries over it.

Be prepared for euphoria.

RUBEN E. GONZALEZ

Buenuelos

1 1/2 cups flour
1 tablespoon baking powder
1 teaspoon salt
1/4 cup lard
1/4 cup milk

Sift flour, baking powder and salt. Cut in lard as for pastry. Add milk and beat by hand. Form dough into balls about the size of an egg. Roll or pat balls paper thin, until they are 8 to 10 inches across. Deep fry until golden brown.

Sprinkle with sugar or pour syrup or honey over them.

Photo – Vic Topmiller

www.ingramcontent.com/pod-product-compliance
Lightning Source LLC
Chambersburg PA
CBHW081508040426
42446CB00017B/3440